WHO AM I?

Who am I?

I am winged and wild, swooping and strong.
I live in the mountains.

WHO AM I?

By Moira Butterfield
Illustrated by Wayne Ford

Belitha Press

First published in the UK in 1998 by
Belitha Press Limited, London House,
Great Eastern Wharf, Parkgate Road,
London SW11 4NQ

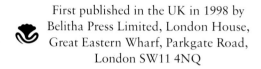

ISBN 1 85561 814 1

British Library Cataloguing in Publication Data for this book
is available from the British Library.

Printed in Hong Kong

Editor: Stephanie Bellwood
Designer: Helen James
Illustrator: Wayne Ford / Wildlife Art Agency
Consultant: Steve Pollock

I'm fierce and fast
and very strong.
My beak is hooked.
My wings are long.
I swoop down low
and soar up high
watching with my beady eye.

Who am I?

Here is my wing

My wings are long,
wide and strong.
I fly around my
mountain home.

Warm air often rises
up from the ground.
I spread my wings
and let the air carry
me high in the sky.

Here is my eye

I can see a long way.
I perch on a rock
or a tree and watch
the ground carefully.

If I see a small animal
I swoop down and
attack it. I am a
very good hunter.

Here are my feet

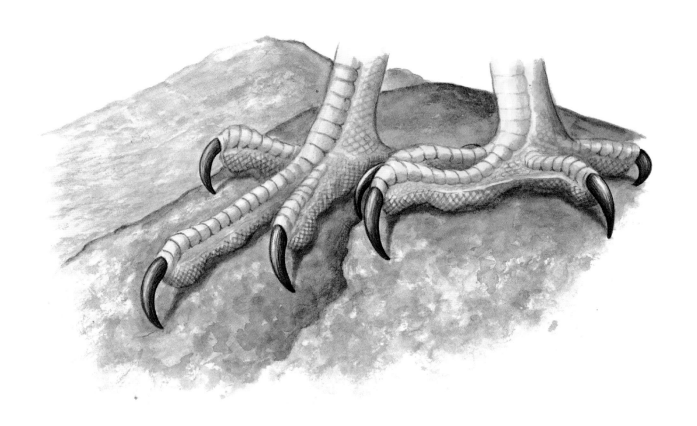

I have long, sharp
claws called talons.
When I catch small
animals I hold them
in my powerful talons.

Sometimes I fly around
looking for animals
to catch. I like to eat
rabbits and small birds.
Can you see any?

Here is my beak

My beak is sharp and hooked at the end. I use it to rip my food into pieces.

If I see a dead sheep or deer I fly down to eat it. I grab chunks of meat with my beak.

Here is my tail

I use it to help
me turn as I fly.
I spread it out
to slow myself
down when I land.

Sometimes other
birds attack me
if I fly near their
home. I turn and
twist easily to escape.

Here is my head

Some of the feathers
on my head and
my neck are golden.
They make my head
shine in the sun.

I can turn my head
a long way round.
This is helpful if I
am looking for food.

Here is my nest

It is called an eyrie. I build it high
up on a cliff or in a tall tree.
My mate lives in it with me.

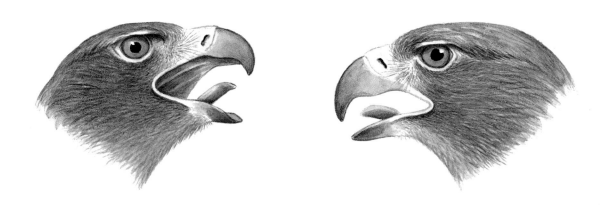

We make loud cries like this...

kee-ar, kee-ar!

Have you guessed who I am?

I am a golden eagle

Point to my...

strong wings

wide tail

hooked beak

sharp talons

golden head

shiny yellow eyes

I am a female eagle.

Here is my baby

I lay a white, speckled egg and sit on it to keep it warm. Then a baby eagle hatches. It is called a chick.

I bring my chick food until it grows big enough to be a fierce, brave hunter like me.

Here is my territory

This is the place where
I live and hunt for food.

Can you see me flying high in the sky?
Look for a fox, three rabbits, four deer
and two big, black birds called ravens.

Here is a map of the world

I live in many
northern parts
of the world.
Can you see the
places where I live?

Can you point to the
place where you live?

The places where
I live are this colour.

Can you answer these questions about me?

What do I use
my tail for?

Why is my hooked
beak useful?

What do I like to eat?

What is my nest called?

Where do I
build my nest?

What kind of
noise do I make?

What do I use
my talons for?

Can you describe the
colour of my feathers?

What is my baby called?

Here are some words to learn about me

beak My mouth. My beak is strong and hard. I use it for tearing up my food.

eyrie My nest. I build it with twigs. I lay eggs and keep my chicks warm in my nest.

hooked Bent over. The end of my beak is sharp and hooked.

hunter An animal that chases and kills other animals to eat.

mate The eagle I live with. I am a female eagle, so I have a male mate.

mountain A high, rocky place. I live in mountains in northern parts of the world.

perch To sit or stand in a tree or on a rock.

speckled Covered in small marks or spots.

swoop To fly quickly downwards.

talons The long, sharp claws on my feet. I hold small animals tightly in my talons.